SandCastle 3

Homonyms

A
Fly
Can
Fly

Kelly Doudna

ABDO
Publishing Company

Published by SandCastle™, an imprint of ABDO Publishing Company, 4940 Viking Drive, Edina, Minnesota 55435.

Printed in the United States.

Photo credits: Comstock, Corbis Images, Diamar, Digital Vision, Eyewire Images, PhotoDisc, Rubberball Productions

Library of Congress Cataloging-in-Publication Data

Doudna, Kelly, 1963-
    A fly can fly / Kelly Doudna.
      p. cm. -- (Homonyms)
    Includes index.
    Summary: Photographs and simple text introduce homonyms, words that are spelled and sound the same but have different meanings.
    ISBN 1-57765-786-1
      1. English language--Homonyms--Juvenile literature. [1. English language--Homonyms.] I. Title.

PE1595 .D74 2002
428.1--dc21

                          2001053324

The SandCastle concept, content, and reading method have been reviewed and approved by a national advisory board including literacy specialists, librarians, elementary school teachers, early childhood education professionals, and parents.

Let Us Know

After reading the book, SandCastle would like you to tell us your stories about reading. What is your favorite page? Was there something hard that you needed help with? Share the ups and downs of learning to read. We want to hear from you! To get posted on the Abdo Publishing Company Web site, send us email at:

sandcastle@abdopub.com

About SandCastle™

Nonfiction books for the beginning reader

- Basic concepts of phonics are incorporated with integrated language methods of reading instruction. Most words are short, and phrases, letter sounds, and word sounds are repeated.

- Book levels are based on the ATOS™ for Books formula. Other considerations for readability include the number of words in each sentence, the number of characters in each word, and word lists based on curriculum frameworks.

- Full-color photography reinforces word meanings and concepts.

- "Words I Can Read" list at the end of each book teaches basic elements of grammar, helps the reader recognize the words in the text, and builds vocabulary.

- Reading levels are indicated by the number of flags on the castle.

SandCastle uses the following definitions for this series:

- Homographs: words that are spelled the same but sound different and have different meanings. *Easy memory tip: "-graph"= same look*

- Homonyms: words that are spelled and sound the same but have different meanings. *Easy memory tip: "-nym"= same name*

- Homophones: words that sound alike but are spelled differently and have different meanings. *Easy memory tip: "-phone"= sound alike*

Look for more SandCastle books in these three reading levels:

Level 1 (one flag)	**Level 2** (two flags)	**Level 3** (three flags)

Grades Pre-K to K 5 or fewer words per page	**Grades K to 1** 5 to 10 words per page	**Grades 1 to 2** 10 to 15 words per page

fence   fence

Homonyms are words that are spelled and sound the same but have different meanings.

Mom and Dad brought us to the fair.

We are having fun.

I hit a fair ball.

I will run fast to first base.

A fan has blades that turn.

It blows air to keep us cool.

Mom comes to my baseball game.

She is my biggest fan.

I wish I did not have to stay inside.

I feel like playing outside.

I take a bite of ice cream.

I can feel it melting in my mouth.

Penguins waddle when they walk.

These three walk in single file.

I do some of my homework on the computer.

I will save this file.

We might get a **fine** if we throw trash on the ground.

I use a pencil to write.

It makes a fine line.

I like to play sports.

Being active makes my body fit.

My kitten is small enough to fit in the bag.

I like to eat hot dogs for lunch.

A hot dog is also called a frank.

Dad gives me a piggyback ride.

His name is Frank.

I look at my friend while I talk to her.

We face each other.

I am at the carnival.

What am I having painted?

(face)

Words I Can Read

Nouns

A noun is a person, place, or thing

air (AIR) p. 8
bag (BAG) p. 17
ball (BAWL) p. 7
base (BAYSS) p. 7
baseball game
   (BAYSS-bawl GAYM)
   p. 9
bite (BITE) p. 11
blades (BLAYDZ) p. 8
body (BOD-ee) p. 16
carnival
   (KAR-nuh-vuhl) p. 21
computer
   (kuhm-PYOO-tur)
   p. 13
face (FAYSS) p. 21
fair (FAIR) p. 6
fan (FAN) pp. 8, 9

fence (FENSS) p. 4
file (FILE) p. 13
fine (FINE) p. 14
frank (FRANGK) p. 18
friend (FREND) p. 20
fun (FUHN) p. 6
ground (GROUND)
   p. 14
homework
   (HOME-wurk) p. 13
homonyms
   (HOM-uh-nimz) p. 5
hot dog (HOT DAWG)
   p. 18
hot dogs
   (HOT DAWGZ) p. 18
ice cream
   (EYESS KREEM) p. 11

kitten (KIT-uhn) p. 17
line (LINE) p. 15
lunch (LUHNCH) p. 18
meanings (MEE-ningz)
   p. 5
mouth (MOUTH) p. 11
name (NAYM) p. 19
pencil (PEN-suhl) p. 15
penguins (PEN-gwinz)
   p. 12
ride (RIDE) p. 19
single file
   (SING-guhl FILE) p. 12
sports (SPORTSS) p. 16
trash (TRASH) p. 14
words (WURDZ) p. 5

Proper Nouns

A proper noun is the name of a
person, place, or thing

Dad (DAD) pp. 6, 19   Frank (FRANGK) p. 19   Mom (MOM) pp. 6, 9

Pronouns

A pronoun is a word that replaces a noun

each other
(EECH UHTH-ur) p. 20
her (HUR) p. 20
I (EYE) pp. 7, 10, 11, 13,
15, 16, 18, 20, 21
it (IT) pp. 8, 11, 15

me (MEE) p. 19
she (SHEE) p. 9
some (SUHM) p. 13
that (THAT) pp. 5, 8
they (THAY) p. 12

this (THISS) p. 13
three (THREE) p. 12
us (UHSS) pp. 6, 8
we (WEE) pp. 6, 14, 20
what (WUHT) p. 21

Verbs

A verb is an action or being word

am (AM) p. 21
are (AR) pp. 5, 6
being (BEE-ing) p. 16
blows (BLOHZ) p. 8
brought (BRAWT) p. 6
called (KAWLD) p. 18
can (KAN) p. 11
comes (KUHMZ) p. 9
did (DID) p. 10
do (DOO) p. 13
eat (EET) p. 18
face (FAYSS) p. 20
feel (FEEL) pp. 10, 11
fence (FENSS) p. 4
fit (FIT) p. 17
get (GET) p. 14
gives (GIVZ) p. 19
has (HAZ) p. 8

have (HAV) pp. 5, 10
having (HAV-ing)
pp. 6, 21
hit (HIT) p. 7
is (IZ) pp. 9, 17, 18, 19
keep (KEEP) p. 8
like (LIKE) pp. 16, 18
look (LUK) p. 20
makes (MAYKSS)
pp. 15, 16
melting (MELT-ing)
p. 11
might (MITE) p. 14
painted (PAYNT-ed)
p. 21
play (PLAY) p. 16
playing (PLAY-ing)
p. 10

run (RUHN) p. 7
save (SAYV) p. 13
sound (SOUND) p. 5
spelled (SPELD) p. 5
stay (STAY) p. 10
take (TAYK) p. 11
talk (TAWK) p. 20
throw (THROH) p. 14
turn (TURN) p. 8
use (YOOZ) p. 15
waddle (WAHD-uhl)
p. 12
walk (WAWK) p. 12
will (WIL) pp. 7, 13
wish (WISH) p. 10
write (RITE) p. 15

Adjectives

An adjective describes something

active (AK-tiv) p. 16
biggest (BIG-est) p. 9
cool (KOOL) p. 8
different (DIF-ur-uhnt)
  p. 5
fair (FAIR) p. 7
fast (FAST) p. 7
fine (FINE) p. 15

first (FURST) p. 7
fit (FIT) p. 16
his (HIZ) p. 19
my (MYE)
  pp. 9, 11, 13, 16, 17, 20
piggyback
  (PIG-ee-bak) p. 19
same (SAYM) p. 5

small (SMAWL) p. 17
these (THEEZ) p. 12
this (THISS) p. 13

Adverbs

An adverb tells how, when, or where
something happens

also (AWL-soh) p. 18
enough (i-NUF) p. 17

fast (FAST) p. 7
inside (in-SIDE) p. 10

outside (out-SIDE) p. 10

12.95